The adventures of Norman the Ninja

Norman Smith is a shy six year old boy, who dreams everyday about being a superhero, just like the ones on TV.

Then, one day it all changed when a leaflet dropped through the letterbox.

Follow Norman's amazing adventures whilst learning valuable life skills. Each page gives our little ninjas a positive saying to work with during their normal day

It costs nothing to be nice.

Three months had gone by since Norman Smith became a Little Ninja, he was such a different little boy now, full of confidence and always wanting to help other people. Today he woke with excitement as today was the day he would be attending his first grading, (in martial arts you get graded and given belts to show your improvement) today.

Norman had been dreaming of this day, as he was going to be graded for his white belt, this is the first belt on the list, its like a test to see if you know all the moves you have been taught. Norman so wanted to be a black belt like Sensei Ken

When Norman attended the little Ninjas class, he would always notice and admire how good and kind the little ninjas were, especially the ones who had belts of different colours. Norman asked in what order to the belts go in

Emily Sensei Ken's granddaughter explained to Norman that they go, white, yellow, orange, green, red, blue, purple, purple one, brown, brown one and then black belt "Wow" said Norman, it is like a rainbow.

Norman realised he had a lot to learn and a lot of work to do. To gain his belts. He kept saying to himself, "Look, listen and think" that way he knew he would learn and gain "K" nowledge. and that was power

The clock struck 10 O'clock and Sensei Ken asked the Little Ninjas to line up Norman could not stop smiling, he was hopefully going to pass his white belt grading after the class.

Are you ready? Shouted Sensei Ken, everyone replied at the top of their voices "we were born ready!" 3,2,1" shouted Sensei Ken, the little ninjas shouted, "feet together, hands by your side, head up, left leg, right leg, bow, Norman loved bowing the class on it made him feel like a warrior superhero.

During the class Sensei Ken taught the Little Ninjas, how to Block, (that is stopping someone from hitting you by raising your arm) if someone went to hit you, Norman had seen superhero's doing this on films, this only made Norman more Determined to try his hardest and learn as much as possible

11 o'clock came and Sensei Ken shouted "Little ninjas line up" Norman was excited and worried as the time for his grading had arrived

3,2,1 and the Little Ninjas, shouted back "feet together, hands by your side, head up, left leg, right leg, bow, (watch you don't bang your head) left leg, right leg, bow" but there was one thing different! Everyone shouted "thank you" as Sensei Ken said "it costs nothing to be nice

After saying goodbye to all the students and parents, Sensei Ken shouted, okay little ninjas who are taking their white belt grading Come here please. Everyone looked worried and nervous as they all wanted to pass their white belt grading. Sensei Ken, said right "who would like to go first"

Norman confidently put his hand up and shouted, "me please". Sensei Ken said "well done Norman" the other little ninjas sat down by the parents and waited for their turn.

Norman lined up facing Sensei Ken, feeling nervous, but Sensei Ken Said "Norman just relax, all I want you to do is copy me, using your inner power and strength. Every punch and kick you do, I want you to I want you to punch and kick as hard as a superhero, Norman needed no further encouragement.

Sensei Ken said" Norman are you ready "Norman shouted, "back really loud "Yes Sensei" Wow said Sensei Ken that was powerful. They both bowed to each other and Sensei Ken started a series of moves, starting with his fighting stance (this is how You stand when preparing to fight) Norman knew this after his lessons and watching his superhero's

The grading went on for some time, with Norman copying Sensei Ken's moves including punches and Kicks. Norman took a little look over to his mum and dad with a proud smile they gave Norman a big smile and a big thumbs up

Sensei Ken said right Norman last three moves. Inside Kick, outside kick and then inside and outside kick together, Norman knew these moves and that they Were Thai boxing moves. Sensei Ken started, then it was Norman's turn, he launched powerful loud kicks filling the dojo with the noise of his kicks.

Sensei Ken, said wow Norman you are powerful fast and loud Once he had finished, Sensei Ken said "bow" which they both did. Norman was so excited and exhausted as he put so much effort and power into his moves, this was something Sensei Ken always said.

Sensei Ken went over to his bag and produced a white belt, Norman grinned from ear to ear. Well done said Sensei Ken You have passed, but not only passed you have achieved an A mark grading which is fantastic, something to be extremely Proud of. Well done Norman, everyone in the dojo clapped and shouted well done Norman.

Sensei Ken then showed Norman how to tie his belt, which
Is quite complicated, but Sensei Ken said do not worry,
you
Will soon learn how to do it. After both bowing to each
other Norman ran back to his parents who were so excited
and happy That Norman had passed his white belt

Norman ran to the door and opened it shouting "look mum, dad! I am not just a little Ninja I am a white belt little ninja. Normans mum and dad said" you certainly are now Norman we are so proud of you.

The other Little Ninjas took their gradings and passed. Sensei Ken congratulated everyone for the strong effort, strength and attitude. Norman had realised by now that what Sensei Ken always said" It costs nothing to be nice was right

Norman without asking put the remaining chairs and equipment away and, with a great big smile on his face, held the doors open for the mums and dads

Norman really felt like a superhero now, he had gained his white belt, one step closer to achieving a black belt like Sensei Ken

Norman ran to the door and opened it shouting "look mum, dad! I am not just a little Ninja I am a white belt little ninja. Normans mum and dad said" you certainly are now Norman we are so proud of you.

Write down below what you have learnt from this book.

Write down below what are you going to do to become like Norman?

Write down below how you can help your Mum and Dad?

What do you want to be when you grow up?

Printed in Great Britain
by Amazon